Explore the Inca Empire

Candice Ransom

Lerner Publications ◆ Minneapolis

Copyright © 2026 by Lerner Publishing Group, Inc.

All rights reserved. International copyright secured. No part of this book may be reproduced, stored in a retrieval system, or transmitted in any form or by any means—electronic, mechanical, photocopying, recording, or otherwise—without the prior written permission of Lerner Publishing Group, Inc., except for the inclusion of brief quotations in an acknowledged review.

Lerner Publications Company
An imprint of Lerner Publishing Group, Inc.
241 First Avenue North
Minneapolis, MN 55401 USA

For reading levels and more information, look up this title at www.lernerbooks.com

Main body text set in Billy Infant Regular. Typeface provided by SparkyType.

Editor: Angel Kidd **Photo Editor:** Angel Kidd

Library of Congress Cataloging-in-Publication Data

Names: Ransom, Candice F., 1952- author
Title: Explore the Inca Empire / Candice Ransom.
Description: Minneapolis, MN : Lerner Publications, 2026. | Series: Lightning bolt books. Early civilizations | Includes bibliographical references and index. | Audience: Ages 6-9 | Audience: Grades 2-3 | Summary: "The Incas ruled a large empire in the fifteenth and sixteenth centuries. From keeping llamas to make clothes to running messages along their long roads, readers will learn about the life of the Incas"— Provided by publisher.
Identifiers: LCCN 2025015087 (print) | LCCN 2025015088 (ebook) | ISBN 9798765689318 library binding | ISBN 9798348029005 paperback | ISBN 9798765696941 epub
Subjects: LCSH: Incas—Juvenile literature
Classification: LCC F3429 .R36 2026 (print) | LCC F3429 (ebook) | DDC 985/.01—dc23/eng/20250528

LC record available at https://lccn.loc.gov/2025015087
LC ebook record available at https://lccn.loc.gov/2025015088

Manufactured in the United States of America
1-1012508-54799-7/24/2025

Table of Contents

Great Empire

The Inca civilization controlled the largest empire in the world in the fifteenth century. A civilization is a group of people who live in an area together and form a community.

The Inca took over other people's lands to build their empire. It stretched from what we now call Columbia to Argentina.

The empire stretched all the way from the Andes Mountains to the Pacific Ocean. The Inca rulers needed a way to control all that territory.

A community called Quechua still lives in the area.

Roads and Palaces

The Inca built roads that covered 25,000 miles (40,200 km). Two main roads went from north to south.

Smaller roads, trails, and rope bridges crossed deserts, mountains, and rivers. **Some of the roads are still in use.**

This Inca bridge is about five hundred years old.

Workers repaired and cleaned the roads and bridges. But they could not travel on them. Only soldiers, nobles, people in government, and messengers could use them.

Emperors were the rulers of the Inca.

The Inca had no written language. Multiple runners delivered messages that they had memorized or recorded with a quipu.

A quipu was a series of cords tied to a main cord. **Knots in the cords had meanings as words and numbers do.**

Runners would jog to the next runner and share the message. Each new runner would pass it on until it was delivered to the right person.

An Inca runner carries a quipu message.

Inca families lived in mud brick houses. Men were farmers, soldiers, or road workers. Women cared for the family and cooked.

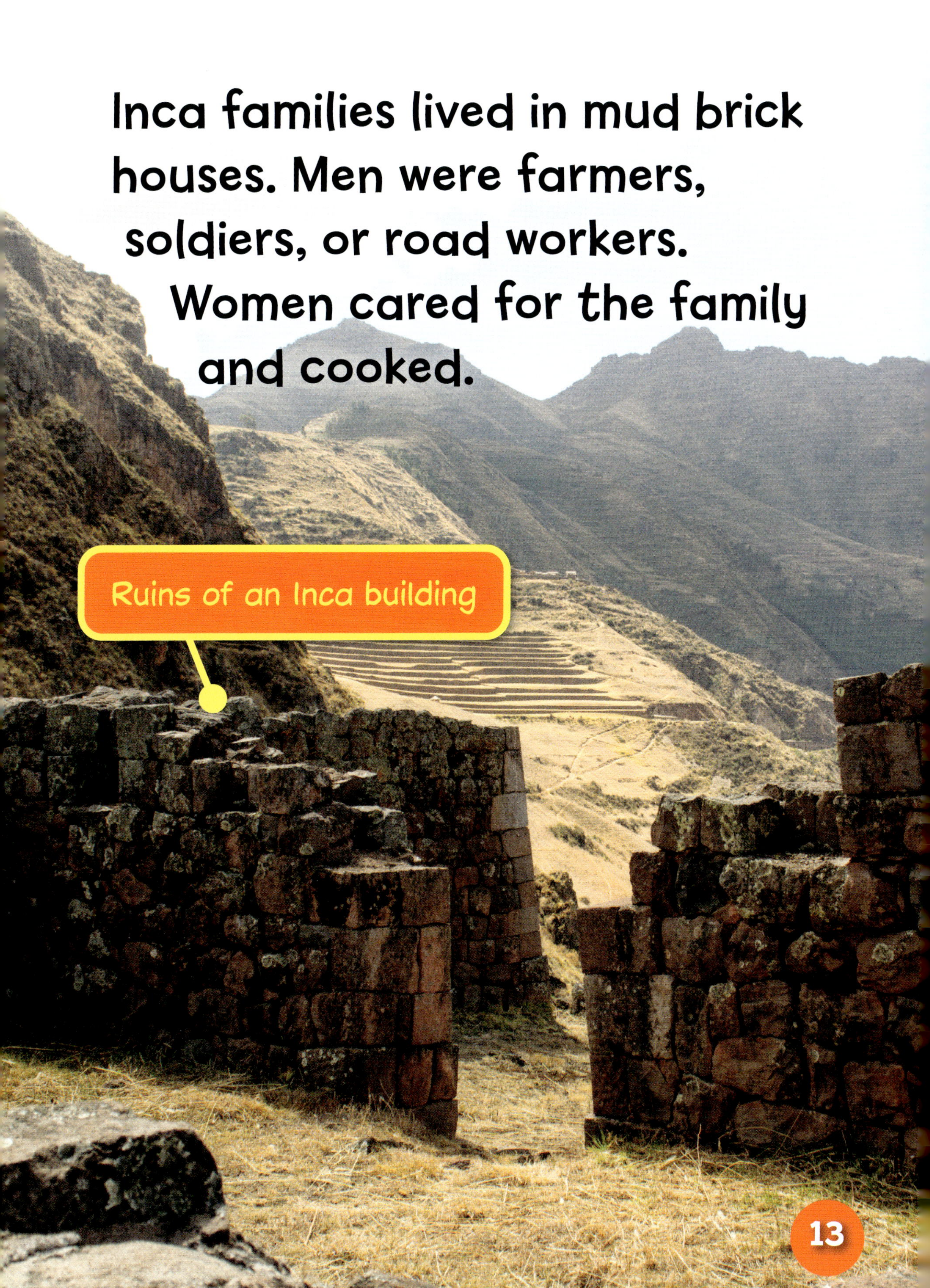

Ruins of an Inca building

Families grew corn, potatoes, and fruit. They raised ducks for food and llamas for wool.

Llamas were important to the empire. They could climb mountains and carry things over long distances. Women also wove llama wool into warm clothes, ponchos, and blankets.

The Inca built palaces and temples from huge stone blocks. Masons carved and stacked the stones. The blocks fit together so tightly that a knife blade could not slide between them.

Inca rulers may have sat at the top of this pyramid.

End of an Empire

In 1532, Spanish explorer Francisco Pizarro arrived with horses, guns, and 260 men. They carried smallpox, a disease that killed thousands of Incan people.

Pizarro wanted gold and land for Spain. The Inca had plenty of both. Pizarro's army attacked the empire's capital, Cuzco.

The Inca made many items out of gold.

Pizarro killed the Inca emperor.

The Inca fought with spears. The Spanish had armor and cannons. In 1572, the last Inca king, Túpac Amaru, was killed. The largest empire at that time was gone.

A Look at Machu Picchu

The Incan city Machu Picchu was hidden in the forest for hundreds of years. The Spanish never knew it was there. In 1911, American explorer Hiram Bingham found the ruins. Today, people from all over the globe climb thousands of steps to visit this ancient city.

Inca Facts

- The Inca were experts at making fabric. Their clothing was more valuable to them than gold.
- The Inca honored their dead by turning them into mummies.
- The Inca spoke a language called Quechua. Some Quechua words are still used in English, such as *puma*, *llama*, and *poncho*.

Glossary

capital: the city where a government is located

empire: a group of nations or peoples under one ruler or government

mason: a worker who builds with cement, stone, or brick

memorize: to learn by heart

noble: a person of high rank

poncho: a blanketlike cloak with an opening for the head

quipu: a series of cords tied to a main cord to record information

smallpox: a dangerous disease

Learn More

Britannica Kids: Inca
https://kids.britannica.com/kids/article/Inca/353286

Britannica Kids: Llama
https://kids.britannica.com/kids/article/llama/353394

Havemeyer, Janie. *A Day in the Inca Empire*. Grasshopper, 2025.

Mitchell, KS. *Machu Picchu*. Focus Readers, 2023.

National Geographic Kids: Inca Civilization
https://kids.nationalgeographic.com/history/article/inca-civilization

Ransom, Candice. *Explore the Aztec Empire*. Lerner Publications, 2026.

Index

Photo Acknowledgments

Image credits: World History Archive/Alamy, p. 4; Laura Westlund/Independent Picture Service, p. 5; Tuul & Bruno Morandi/Getty Images, p. 6; Mac99/Getty Images, p. 7; Connect Images/Alamy, p. 8; ilbusca/Getty Images, pp. 9, 19; Ruben Senor is a traveler, writer, director and photographer/Getty Images, p. 10; andyKRAKOVSKI/Getty Images, p. 11; duncan1890/Getty Images, p. 12; S Pinter/Getty Images, p. 13; Kitti Boonnitrod/Getty Images, p. 14; Posnov/Getty Images, p. 15; imageBROKER/Peter Giovannini/Getty Images, p. 16; clu/Getty Images, p. 17; Sunshine Pics/Alamy, p. 18; agaliza/Getty Images, p. 20.

Cover: Craig Hastings/Getty Images.